DID YOU KNOW?
SPORTS

20 THINGS YOU DIDN'T KNOW ABOUT

FOOTBALL

THEIA LAKE

PowerKiDS press

Published in 2026 by The Rosen Publishing Group, Inc.
2544 Clinton Street, Buffalo, NY 14224

Portions of this work were originally authored by Ryan Nagelhout and published as *20 Fun Facts About Football*. All new material in this edition was authored by Theia Lake.

Editor: Greg Roza
Book Design: Tanya Dellaccio Keeney

Photo Credits: Cover JoeSAPhotos/Shutterstock.com; p. 5 Steve Broer/Shutterstock.com; p. 6 (right) Superstock/Alamy Images; p. 6 (right) MyBestCollection/Shutterstock.com; p. 7 Jim West/Alamy Images; p. 8 https://upload.wikimedia.org/wikipedia/commons/5/50/John_Brallier_1895_W%26J_uniform_cropped.jpg; p. 9 https://upload.wikimedia.org/wikipedia/commons/d/df/Jim_Thorpe_Canton_Bulldogs_1915-20.jpg; p. 10 (left) Eric Glenn/Shutterstock.com; p. 10 (right) WoodysPhotos/Shutterstock.com; p. 11 https://upload.wikimedia.org/wikipedia/commons/b/b9/Chicago_Stadium_1930.jpeg; pp. 12, 27 UPI/Alamy Images; p. 14 Jamie Lamor Thompson/Shutterstock.com; p. 15 fifg/Shutterstock.com; pp. 16, 25 Zuma Press, Inc./Alamy Images; p. 17 AP/AP Images; p. 18 https://upload.wikimedia.org/wikipedia/en/0/07/Filchock-Frank-1945.jpg; p. 19 shocky/Shutterstock.com; p. 20 Sipa USA/Alamy Images; p. 21 Rich Kane Photography/Alamy Images; p. 22 Xinhua/Alamy Images; p. 23 https://upload.wikimedia.org/wikipedia/commons/2/2b/The_Paley_Center_for_Media_%2848155560156%29.jpg; p. 24 https://upload.wikimedia.org/wikipedia/commons/0/07/Gale_sayers_playing.jpg; p. 26 Andre Boutin-Maloney/Alamy Images; p. 29 Cal Sport Media/Alamy Images.

Some of the images in this book illustrate individuals who are models. The depictions do not imply actual situations or events.

Library of Congress Cataloging-in-Publication Data

Names: Lake, Theia, author.
Title: 20 things you didn't know about football / Theia Lake.
Other titles: Twenty things you did not know about football
Description: Buffalo, New York : PowerKids Press, [2026] | Series: Did you know? Sports | Includes index.
Identifiers: LCCN 2025000892 (print) | LCCN 2025000893 (ebook) | ISBN 9781499450361 (lib. bdg.) | ISBN 9781499450354 (paperback) | ISBN 9781499450378 (ebook)
Subjects: LCSH: Football--History--Juvenile literature. | Football--United States--Miscellanea--Juvenile literature.
Classification: LCC GV950.7 .L27 2026 (print) | LCC GV950.7 (ebook) | DDC 796.33209--dc23/eng/20250214
LC record available at https://lccn.loc.gov/2025000892
LC ebook record available at https://lccn.loc.gov/2025000893

Manufactured in the United States of America

CPSIA Compliance Information: Batch #CSPK26. For Further Information contact Rosen Publishing at 1-800-237-9932.

CONTENTS

THE GAME'S ON!

The National Football League (NFL) has been a part of the American sports landscape since 1920. It's one of the most popular sports in the United States and is gaining popularity around the world. It's fun to watch on TV and even more fun to watch from the stands!

But how much do you know about football? Did you know there's a record that can never be broken? Did you know football is different in Canada? Read on to discover the answers to these fun facts and more!

The New England Patriots is one of the NFL's most successful teams. The Patriots play their home games at Gillette Stadium in Foxborough, Massachusetts.

ON THE BALL

DID YOU KNOW?

Footballs today are oval shaped. However, the first footballs were round.

The first game of football was held on November 6, 1869, at Rudgers University in New Jersey. The first ball was similar to a soccer ball. It was hard to carry and very hard to throw. In 1874, the ball became more oval, which made it easier to hold and toss to teammates.

A football is sometimes called a "pigskin." They were originally made from pig bladders, which were hard to keep full of air.

Wilson has made the official game ball for the NFL since 1941. Wilson makes 228 footballs for the Super Bowl alone.

DID YOU KNOW?

Official NFL footballs have been made by the same company for more than 80 years.

The Wilson Sporting Goods introduced their first football design in 1922. After some changes, the **oblong** football began to resemble modern footballs. This design made it even easier to throw, and the importance of passing increased.

IN THE PROS

DID YOU KNOW?

William Walter "Pudge" Heffelfinger was the first "**professional**" football player.

In 1892, Yale University student Heffelfinger was paid $500 by the Allegheny **Athletic** Association (AAA). He helped the AAA beat the Pittsburgh Athletic Club by picking up a **fumble** and running 35 yards for the winning touchdown!

John Brallier (shown here) was the first player to openly and officially turn pro in 1895. He was paid $10 plus expenses to play for Latrobe YMCA against the Jeannette Athletic Club.

In 1963, Thorpe was one of the first 17 players to be inducted into the Pro Football Hall of Fame.

DID YOU KNOW?

The king of Sweden told Jim Thorpe he was the greatest athlete in the world!

Thorpe was a star playing for the Canton Bulldogs and the Carlisle School of Indians team, an all-Native American group that toured the country in the 1910s. Thorpe also won important events at the 1912 Olympic Games. He also played baseball and lacrosse.

THE OLD DAYS OF FOOTBALL

DID YOU KNOW?

The NFL formed in Canton, Ohio.

In 1920, the American Professional Football Association formed in Canton, Ohio. This league later became the NFL. The Canton Bulldogs were formed in 1904 and were one of the most successful early NFL teams, winning back-to-back NFL titles in 1922 and 1923.

The Bulldogs only lasted until 1926. However, in 1963, the Football Hall of Fame opened in Canton and has grown ever since.

PRO FOOTBALL HALL OF FAME CANTON, OHIO

This photograph from 1930 shows the inside of the Chicago Stadium before a Chicago Blackhawks game.

DID YOU KNOW?

The Chicago Bears once played on an in-door hockey rink due to bad weather!

In 1932, the Bears won a **playoff** game, 9 to 0, against the Portsmouth Spartans inside Chicago Stadium. Freezing temperatures and a **blizzard** meant the game couldn't be played outside. The "field" was only 80 yards (73 m) long and was 30 feet (9 m) narrower than a regular field!

COMING TOGETHER

DID YOU KNOW?

Today's NFL is two different leagues that merged, or joined together.

In 1959, the American Football League (AFL) was started by Lamar Hunt. The AFL had eight teams, which were rivals with the NFL for fans and even players. Teams from the two leagues first played one another in Super Bowl I in 1967.

The two leagues fully merged in 1970, with the NFL becoming the National Football Conference (NFC) and the AFL becoming the American Football Conference (AFC).

LAMAR HUNT

THE AFL/NFL MERGER

NFL TEAMS

San Francisco
Los Angeles
Dallas
New Orleans
St. Louis
Minnesota
Green Bay
Chicago
Detroit
Atlanta
Washington
Philadelphia

AFL TEAMS

Oakland
San Diego
Denver
Kansas City
Houston
Cincinnati
Miami
Buffalo
Boston

TEAMS IN BOTH LEAGUES

New York

TEAMS THAT WENT FROM THE NFL TO THE AFC

Cleveland
Pittsburg
Baltimore

NAME GAME

DID YOU KNOW?

Many football teams "stole" their name from popular baseball teams.

From 1933 to 1940, the Pittsburgh Steelers were named after the Major League Baseball (MLB) team the Pirates. The New York Giants are named after a baseball team that moved to San Francisco, California, in 1958. They were sometimes called the New York "Football" Giants to avoid confusion.

The New York Jets were almost named the Dodgers, after an MLB team that once played in nearby Brooklyn.

In 1975, Seattle picked "Seahawks" out of more than 1,700 possible names sent in by fans. Other names included Skippers, Pioneers, Lumberjacks, and Seagulls.

DID YOU KNOW?

Some fans have picked their own team's name!

Many teams, including the Oakland Raiders, San Diego Chargers, and Miami Dolphins, held contests to pick their team names. Jaguars were named by a fan even though jaguars aren't native to Jacksonville!

FOOTBALL KICKERS

DID YOU KNOW?

An NFL kicker with no toes once kicked a 63-yard field goal!

In 1970, The New Orleans's Saints player Tom Dempsey kicked a record-setting field goal in a 19–17 win over the Detroit Lions. Dempsey was born without toes on his right foot and without fingers on his right hand. Dempsey played 11 seasons in the NFL!

JUSTIN TUCKER

Dempsey's record lasted until 2013, when Denver Bronco's kicker Matt Prater kicked a 64-yard field goal. The current record—66 yards—was set by Baltimore Raven's kicker Justin Tucker.

Moseley, shown here, played for Washington for 13 seasons. He also played for the Philadelphia Eagles, Houston Oilers, and Cleveland Browns.

DID YOU KNOW?

Mark Moseley is the only kicker to win the NFL's Most **Valuable** Player (MVP) award.

Moseley won the award playing for Washington in 1982. He made 20 of 21 field goals during the season. That's an amazing 95.2 percent! Moseley is the only kicker to ever win the MVP award.

UNBEATABLE!

DID YOU KNOW?

Washington quarterback Frank Filchock set a record that can never be broken!

On October 15, 1939, during a game against Pittsburgh, Filchock threw a 99-yard touchdown pass to Andy Farkas. The record has been matched more than 10 times since, but no one will ever throw a longer touchdown in the NFL.

It's not possible to throw a longer touchdown pass because the field is only 100 yards long and the ball can't be snapped, or passed back to the quarterback, from the goal line.

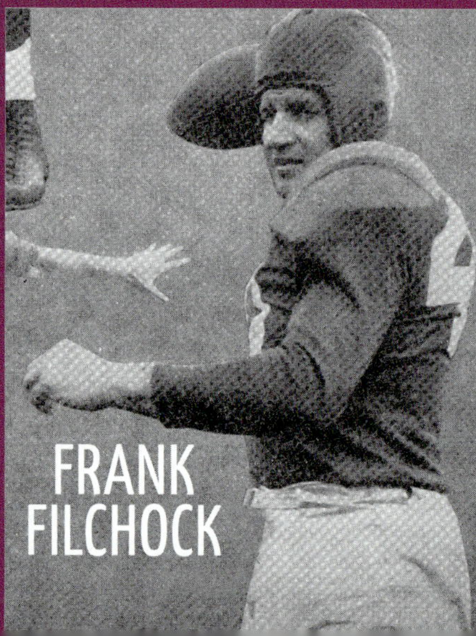

THE LONGEST TOUCHDOWNS

LONGEST PUNT RETURN

Robert Bailey

Los Angeles Rams vs.
New Orleans Saints
Oct. 23, 1994 (103 yards)

LONGEST INTERCEPTION RETURN

Ed Reed

Baltimore Ravens vs.
Philadelphia Eagles
Nov. 23, 2008 (107 yards)

LONGEST FUMBLE RETURN

Jack Tatum

Oakland Raiders vs.
Green Bay Packers
Sept. 24, 1972

Aeneas Williams

Arizona Cardinals vs.
Washington Commanders
Nov. 5, 2000 (104 yards)

LONGEST KICKOFF RETURN

Cordarrelle Patterson

Minnesota Vikings vs.
Green Bay Packers
Oct. 27, 2013 (109 yards)

LONGEST MISSED FIELD GOAL RETURN

Antonio Cromartie

San Diego Chargers vs.
Minnesota Vikings
Nov. 5, 2007 (109 yards)

BEST OF THE BEST

DID YOU KNOW?

Only one player has won 7 NFL **championship** games—otherwise known as the Super Bowl.

Tom Brady has appeared in 10 Super Bowls! He led the New England Patriots to 6 Super Bowl wins between 2001 and 2018, and then did it one more time with the Tampa Bay Buccaneers in 2021.

Brady was voted MVP for 5 of the 10 Super Bowls he played in.

Smith led the Bills to four straight Super Bowls (1991–1994), but they came away without a win.

DID YOU KNOW?

Only one player reached 200 sacks over the course of his career.

Bruce Smith played defensive end for the Buffalo Bills from 1985 to 1999, and for the Washington Commanders from 2000 to 2003. During that time, Smith sacked the other team's quarterback 200 times!

SUPER SUPER BOWL FACTS

DID YOU KNOW?

Only one team has ever had "home-field advantage" in a Super Bowl.

The Super Bowl is held in a different stadium every year. Only one team has played in a Super Bowl at their own stadium—the 2020–2021 Tampa Bay Buccaneers. The Bucs, lead by quarterback Tom Brady, beat the Kansas City Chiefs 31 to 9.

The Buccaneers play in Raymond James Stadium, which can hold nearly 70,000 fans. The 2020–2021 Super Bowl, however, only had a crowd of 25,000 fans due to the COVID-19 pandemic.

The Paley Center had searched for tape of the first Super Bowl for more than 20 years!

DID YOU KNOW?

Film footage of the first Super Bowl was lost until 2005!

Two networks—CBS and NBC—broadcast the game, but they both taped over copies of the game between the NFL's Green Bay Packers and the AFL's Kansas City Chiefs. The Paley Center for Media got a copy from a man who found a tape in a family member's attic!

HALL OF FAMERS

DID YOU KNOW?

The youngest player ever inducted in the NFL Hall of Fame was only 32.

Gayle Sayers was a running back with the Chicago Bears from 1965 to 1971. He wowed players, coaches, and fans with his incredible speed and ability to avoid tackles. Sayers missed part of the 1968–1969 season with a knee injury. He made a comeback in 1969, but decided to retire young after more injuries.

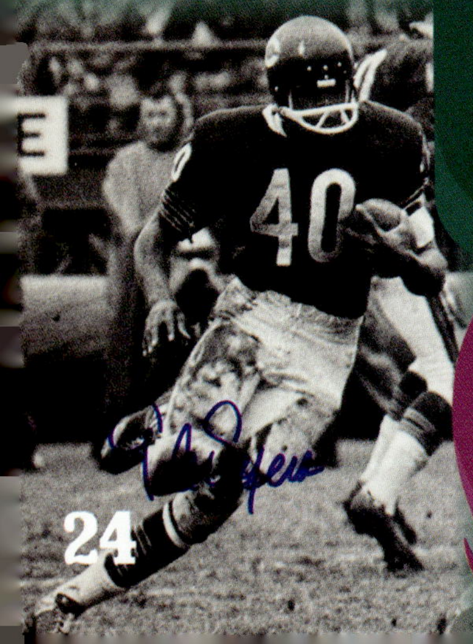

Regarding his success at running back, Sayers famously said: "Just give me 18 inches of daylight. That's all I need."

Sobol was 94 when he was inducted into the Hall of Fame in 2011. He died in 2015 at the age of 98.

DID YOU KNOW?

The oldest person ever inducted in the Hall of Fame wasn't even a player.

Ed Sabol was the founder of NFL Films. He **revolutionized** sports broadcasting and is credited with many firsts, including slow-motion replays and **blooper reels**. He helped draw in fans by bringing a movie-maker's eye to football.

CANADIAN FOOTBALL

DID YOU KNOW?

Football fields in the Canadian Football League (CFL) are bigger than NFL fields.

An NFL playing field is 100 yards long and 53.3 yards wide. Midfield in the NFL is the 50-yard line. A CFL field is 110 yards long, which makes the 55-yard line midfield! A CFL field is also 65 yards wide.

NFL end zones are 10 yards deep. CFL end zones are twice as large, and the goalposts are actually in the end zone. This means the uprights sit on the goal line.

During his 20-year career, Flutie played for 8 professional football teams: New Jersey Generals, Chicago Bears, New England Patriots (2 different times), BC Lions, Calgary Stampeders, Toronto Argonauts, Buffalo Bills, and San Diego Chargers.

DID YOU KNOW?

The CFL's greatest player is an American

In 2006, a committee of CFL players, coaches, and members of the media voted on the CFL's greatest players of all time. Quarterback Doug Flutie, from Maryland, was voted #1! Flutie won three Gray Cups (CFL championship game), three Grey Cup MVP awards, and was voted CFL most outstanding player 6 times.

THE EVOLUTION OF FOOTBALL

The rules of football have changed a lot over the decades. Did you know that the touchdown wasn't always worth 6 points? It was actually worth 4 points until 1898, when it was changed to 5. It wasn't worth 6 points until 1912! A field goal was worth 4 points until 1909, when it was dropped to the 3-point play we know today.

As football continues to grow, new rules are added, and the game continues to change. Maybe the facts you know about the game now will soon be history!

The NFL updates rules often. Rules change to keep players safer, and to make the game more exciting.

GLOSSARY

athletic: Having to do with sports or exercising.

blizzard: A severe snowstorm with high winds and low visibility.

blooper reel: A collection of mistakes or outtakes shown to amuse the audience.

championship: A contest to find out who's the best player or team in a sport.

fumble: To drop the football during a play.

induct: To officially make a person a member of a group or organization.

oblong: Longer in one direction than in the other.

pandemic: A widespread outbreak of an illness.

playoff: Having to do with games played after the regular season to decide who plays in the championship game.

professional: Having to do with something done for money.

revolutionize: To change greatly or completely.

valuable: Important.

FOR MORE INFORMATION

BOOKS

Blue, Tyler. *Stars of the NFL*. New York, NY: Abbeville Press, 2023.

Storden, Tom. *Big-Time Football Records*. Mankato, MN: Capstone Press, 2021.

WEBSITES

National Football League
nfl.com
Get schedules and more information about the NFL on its official site.

Pro Football Hall of Fame
profootballhof.com
Learn more about the greats of the game on the Hall of Fame website.

Pro Football Reference
pro-football-reference.com
Find facts, stats, and more about your favorite players and teams here.

Publisher's note to educators and parents: Our editors have carefully reviewed these websites to ensure that they are suitable for students. Many websites change frequently, however, and we cannot guarantee that a site's future contents will continue to meet our high standards of quality and educational value. Be advised that students should be closely supervised whenever they access the internet.

INDEX